D0848436

# THE LITTLE HOUSE BOOKS
## By Laura Ingalls Wilder

LITTLE HOUSE
*Laura Ingalls Wilder*

# The
# Laura Ingalls Wilder
# SONGBOOK

*Favorite Songs from the* LITTLE HOUSE *Books*

COMPILED AND EDITED BY EUGENIA GARSON
ILLUSTRATED BY GARTH WILLIAMS
ARRANGED FOR PIANO AND GUITAR BY
HERBERT HAUFRECHT

HarperCollins*Publishers*

THE LAURA INGALLS WILDER SONGBOOK
Original text copyright © 1968 by Eugenia Garson
Musical arrangements copyright © 1968 by Herbert Haufrecht
Illustrations copyright 1953 by Garth Williams
Illustrations copyright renewed 1981 by Garth Williams
HarperCollins®, 🏠®, and Little House® are trademarks of HarperCollins Publishers Inc.
All rights reserved. Printed in the United States of America. No part of this book may be used or reproduced in any manner whatsoever without written permission except in the case of brief quotations embodied in critical articles and reviews. For information address HarperCollins Children's Books, a division of HarperCollins Publishers, 10 East 53rd Street, New York, NY 10022.
Library of Congress Catalog Card Number: 68-24327
ISBN 0-06-027036-5

# TABLE OF CONTENTS

# PREFACE

Laura Ingalls Wilder's memories were filled with the songs of her girlhood, and so it was natural that music should have played an important part in the Little House books, her warmly glowing firsthand account of family life in pioneer days. From her earliest years when Laura, her parents, her elder sister Mary, and Baby Carrie lived in a log house on the edge of the Big Woods in Wisconsin, Pa sang and played his fiddle for them. When Pa and Ma—Charles and Caroline Ingalls—packed up the covered wagon that was to carry them all farther west, the fiddle in its box was laid carefully between pillows. Its tunes lulled Laura to sleep beside the family campfires all across the plains of Kansas and into Indian country.

After a year in a log cabin on the prairie, the wagon moved them again, this time to Minnesota. Living first in a sod house dug from the banks of Plum Creek, then in the new home Pa had built nearby, Laura and Mary went to school and church for the first time. It was during this year that Mary lost her sight as the result of scarlet fever.

Another long trip, now with a new baby sister, Grace, brought them to a railroad builders' camp in Dakota Territory, where Pa became a railroader for a time. When work stopped for the winter, the Ingalls family stayed on in the surveyors' house. Here they were isolated for months until the arrival of neighbors—Mr. and Mrs. Boast—brought them company and the enjoyment of song-filled evenings.

In the spring, Pa filed his claim for a homestead near the new townsite of De Smet, South Dakota, and put up the first building in town. Then came the grim experience of the snowbound winter when Almanzo Wilder, Laura's future husband, risked his life to bring wheat to the starving settlers. Later the family settled down to summers in a claim shanty on the prairie and sheltered winters in town. While Laura taught school and helped with Mary's expenses at a college for the blind, she was being courted by Almanzo. As the eighth book of the saga concludes, Laura and Almanzo marry and go to live in a little house of their own.

There had been music of many kinds along the way: the merry tunes at Grandpa's dance back in Wisconsin, Ma's gentle hymns during lonely prairie evenings, Cousin Lena's songs at Silver Lake, and the choruses at the singing class where Almanzo was Laura's escort. Church and Sunday school, revival meetings, and patriotic celebrations had their part, as did the "Literaries"—evening gatherings that took place when the little settlement of De Smet began to grow into a community. And in hard times or good there had always been Pa's songs and the voice of the fiddle, echoing longest of all.

*Little House in the Big Woods* was published in 1932; as a children's librarian I welcomed it not only as a wonderful, true story but as a reminder of the basic values so greatly needed in that time of economic depression. As I shared each succeeding volume with the boys and girls in the library, there came repeated comments and questions about the songs that were so often mentioned in the text. Favorites were greeted with delighted recognition; others were tantalizing because they were so elusive. Surely they were as real as everything else in the books! Sometimes songs were available but difficult for young people to play; sometimes words and melodies could not be found, nor was information about them easy to locate. Finally I decided to make a thorough study of all the songs that played a part in the Little House series.

The undertaking proved to be lengthy, interesting, and unexpectedly complex. Reference works on folk, religious, and popular music were consulted. The many subdivisions in these fields made it necessary to go through scores of volumes in order to winnow a few items of information. Some songs had never been widely known; others had attained enormous popularity in their day, only to pass into obscurity and the files of music libraries and collections; a few were known by several titles. Authors and composers were not always correctly identified; hymns were sung to many different tunes; reprinting brought changes in words and melody; and folk songs had countless versions.

Early sheet music, hymnals, song albums, and broadsides were examined and compared. Line-by-line collation was necessary where neither title nor first line was known—indeed, many older books had no indexes at all. Eventually it was possible to trace almost all the songs, with verified related data, and a generous selection appears here.

Many of Mrs. Wilder's songs were handed down through oral tradition, and her texts sometimes differed from the originals. In almost every instance her wording and punctuation have been followed. In the case of a few of the longer songs, some stanzas have been dropped. Whenever information about the song, composer, or lyricist was available, I have included a brief note above the music. This is followed by a few sentences indicating where each song appears in the Little House series. The title of the book and the number of the page on which the song first occurs are also given. Titles are abbreviated as follows:

| LHBW | *Little House in the Big Woods* |
| LHP | *Little House on the Prairie* |
| FB | *Farmer Boy* |
| BPC | *On the Banks of Plum Creek* |
| SSL | *By the Shores of Silver Lake* |
| LW | *The Long Winter* |
| LTP | *Little Town on the Prairie* |
| HGY | *These Happy Golden Years* |

The collection offers a fascinating cross section of songs that went westward with the pioneers. There are airs deeply rooted in the Scottish and English folk tradition, as well as some with a native homespun quality. A number of these tunes were used for dancing or as singing games to be sung and stepped to without music at "play parties" in areas where, for religious reasons, dancing was frowned upon. There are patriotic songs, sentimental ballads, and rhythmic minstrel-show and music-hall melodies. Old hymns are included together with the gospel songs of the nineteenth-century revivalists. The singing school, where people sang together the music they had taken pleasure in learning, is recalled, as are the "singing families" whose concert tours were so successful during the 1840's and 1850's.

The individuality of this widely varied material, ranging from intricate choral settings to single-staff manuscript notation, has been admirably expressed in Herbert Haufrecht's completely new arrangements, which succeed in capturing the spirit of the originals while making them invitingly easy to play and sing.

Grateful acknowledgment of their helpful cooperation is made to the librarians in the Music and Copyright Divisions of the Library of Congress, particularly to Mrs. Rae Korson of the Archive of Folk Song; the Music Departments of The Free Library of Philadelphia and The Buffalo and Erie County Public Library of Buffalo, New York; the Salvation Army Library and the Union Theological Seminary Library in New York City, with special thanks to the staffs of the American History and Music Reference Divisions of the New York Public Library, where most of the work was done; and to Mr. and Mrs. L. D. Lichty, Curators of the Laura Ingalls Wilder Home and Museum in Mansfield, Missouri. Appreciation is also due the late Sigmund Spaeth, author of *A History of Popular Music in America*, James J. Fuld, author of *The Book of World-Famous Music*, and the many other authorities on American music whose published works, too numerous to mention individually, are of incalculable value to the collector.

E. G.

# Home and Memories

# The Beacon-Light of Home

*Words by George F. St. Clair • Music by H. M. Estabrooke • 1879*

*After the Ingalls family had settled into their little claim shanty near De Smet, they rested outdoors in the beautiful spring evening. Darkness was falling softly on the prairie, and the stars came out one by one over the huge sky. Pa felt like music, and this is the song he played.*

SSL, *page 265*

1. When the stars are bright-ly beam-ing, And the sigh-ing winds are still, When
far than gold or glo-ry Is that cot-tage thatched and old, Where

twi - light shad - ows hov - er o'er the lea,  There's a
ros - es bud and blos - som round the door,  For a

ti - ny can - dle gleam - ing From the cot - tage 'neath the hill,  And I
wom - an dwells with - in it With a heart as pure as gold,  And her

know that lit - tle bea - con shines for me.  I can
love is all my own for - ev - er - more.  When the

see its cheer - ful glim - mer From my boat down in the bay,  When
wea - ry day is o - ver And the world has gone to rest,  When my

all a-round the waves are white with foam,
lit-tle bark is danc-ing o'er the foam,

As__ a
Like a

bright-ly o'er the wa-ters Comes its sun-ny lit-tle ray,
dove at night re-turn-ing To the shel-ter of her nest,

A
Seeks my

*for Chorus
repeat verse
to Fine*

to-ken and a mes-sage sweet from home.
heart a-gain the bea-con-light of home.

2. Dear-er

# The Floating Scow of Old Virginia

*Words and Music by Charles T. White • 1847*

Charles T. White was a celebrated African-American singer and composer.
*Pa came into the shanty with an armful of wood and said: "This wind takes your breath away. Soon as I can thaw out my fingers, we'll have a tune to drown the yowl of that wind." But when Ma heard the music, she cried: "For pity's sakes! I'd as soon listen to the wind."*

LW, *page* 42

1. The float - ing scow of old\_ Vir - gin - ia I worked from day\_ to day,\_\_\_\_\_ A -
2. Oh, if_____ I were young\_ a - gain, I'd lead\_ a dif - ferent life,\_\_\_\_\_ Lay
3. Oh, when\_ I'm dead and gone\_ to rest, Lay the old ban - jo by\_ my side,\_\_\_\_\_ Let the

rak - ing a - mong the oys - ter beds, To me — it was — but
up — some mon - ey and buy — some land, And take Di - nah for — my
'pos-sum and 'coon to the fu - ner - al go For they were my on - ly

play. But now — I'm old and fee - ble too, I
wife. But now — I'm get - ting old — and gray, I
pride. Then in soft — re - pose I'll take — my sleep, And

can - not work an - y more. — Oh, car - ry me back to
can - not work an - y more. — Oh, car - ry me back to
I'll dream for - ev - er - more. — You car - ried me back to

old Vir - gin - ia, To the old ___ Vir - gin - ia shore. _____
old Vir - gin - ia, To the old ___ Vir - gin - ia shore. _____
old Vir - gin - ia, To the old ___ Vir - gin - ia shore. _____

**Chorus**

Oh, car - ry me back to old Vir - gin - ia, To old Vir - gin - ia shore, Oh, ___

car - ry me back to old Vir - gin - ia, To old ___ Vir - gin - ia shore. _____

17

# Ben Bolt

*Words by Dr. Thomas Dunn English • Music by Nelson Kneass • 1848*

Dr. English never received payment for this immensely popular song, and the musical accompaniment he wrote for it has been forgotten. The present melody is based on an old German tune.

*When Mr. and Mrs. Boast settled in at Silver Lake, their voices rounded out the family's evenings of song. This was a favorite selection.* SSL, *page 213*

1. Oh, do you re-mem-ber sweet Al - ice, Ben Bolt, Sweet
2. Oh, do you re-mem-ber the wood,_ Ben Bolt, Near the
3. Oh, do you re-mem-ber the school,_ Ben Bolt, And the

Al - ice, with eyes _ so brown, Who wept with de - light when you
green sun - ny slope of the hill, Where oft we have sung 'neath its
Mas - ter so kind and so true, And the lit - tle nook by the

gave her a smile, And trem-bled with fear __ at your frown? In the
wide spread-ing shade, And kept time to the click __ of the mill? The
clear run-ning brook, Where we gath-er'd the flow-'rs as they grew? On the

old church-yard in the val-ley, Ben Bolt, In a cor-ner ob-scure and a-
mill has gone to de-cay, __ Ben Bolt, And a qui-et now reigns all a-
Mas-ter's grave grows the grass, Ben Bolt, And the run-ning lit-tle brook is now

lone, They have fit-ted a slab of __ gran-ite so gray, And sweet
round, See, the old rus-tic porch, with its ros-es so sweet, Lies __
dry, And of all __ the friends who were school-mates then, There re-

Al - ice lies un - der the stone;
scat - ter'd and fal - len to the ground;
mains, Ben, but you _ and _ I.

They have fit - ted a slab of _
See, the old rus - tic porch, with its
And of all _ the friends who were

gran - ite so gray, And sweet Al - ice lies un - der the stone.
ros - es so sweet, Lies _ scat - ter'd and fal - len to the ground.
school - mates then, There re - mains, Ben, but you _ and _ I.

# Keep the Horseshoe over the Door

*Words and Music by J. P. Skelly • 1880*

Skelly, a plumber by trade, also wrote popular songs of many types.
*Over the door of the brand-new claim shanty Pa hung his rifle and a bright, new horseshoe.*
*Later when he sang about the good luck this would bring, Ma said: "It sounds rather*
*heathenish to me, Charles."*                                    SSL, *page 284*

1. We — jour - ney a - long quite con - tent - ed with life, And try to live peace - ful with all; _____ We — keep our-selves free from all trou - ble and
2. The — horse-shoe is luck - y, that's what they all say, It keeps out the spir - it of wrong; _____ It — brings in the fai - ries at night and at
3. If you're start - ing in life with a sweet lit - tle wife, And want to be hap - py and gay, _____ Just — get an old horse-shoe to hang on the

**Chorus**

Keep the horse-shoe hung o-ver the door, _____ It will bring you good luck ev-er - more; _____ If you want to be hap-py and free from all care, Keep the horse-shoe hung o-ver the door. _____

# Life Let Us Cherish

*Words and Music by Hans Georg Nägeli • 1796*

Early sheet music attributes this to Mozart; however, it is actually the work of
Hans Georg Nägeli, a Swiss music educator and publisher.
*When grasshoppers ate the crops so that Pa had to walk back east to get a job, this was the
last song he played before putting away the fiddle.*          BPC, *page 211*

*D.C. al Fine*

toil and care, Why choose the ran - kling thorn to wear, And
at - mos-phere, And fork - éd light - nings rend the air, The

heed - less by the lil - y stray Which blos - soms in the way.
sun re - sumes his sil - ver crest, And smiles a - down the west.

3. The genial seasons soon are o'er,
Then let us ere we quit this shore
Contentment seek; it is life's zest,
The sunshine of the breast.

(Chorus)

4. Away with every toil and care,
And cease the rankling thorn to wear,
With manful hearts life's conflict meet
Till death sounds the retreat.

(Chorus)

# Oft in the Stilly Night

*Words by Thomas Moore • Traditional Scottish Tune • 1815*

A pensive melody that appeared in Moore's *Selection of Popular National Airs.*
This song was one of Abraham Lincoln's favorites.

*Toward the end of a lively musical evening, Pa would play some old tunes like this one "to go to sleep on," he said.*

SSL, *page 213*

**Slow**

1. Oft in the still-y night, Ere slum-ber's chain has
2. When I re-mem-ber all The friends so link'd to-

bound ___ me, Sweet mem-'ry brings the light Of
geth-er, I've seen a-round me fall Like

oth-er days a-round me. The smiles, the tears, of
leaves in win-ter weath-er, I feel like one who

boy - hood's years, The words of love then spo - ken; The
treads a - lone Some ban - quet hall de - sert - ed,

eyes that shone, now dimmed and gone, The cheer - ful hearts now bro - ken.
lights are fled, whose gar - lands dead, And all but he de - part - ed.

**Chorus**

Thus in the still -y night, Ere slum - ber's chain hath bound me,

Sad mem - 'ry brings the light Of oth - er days a - round me.

# Rock Me to Sleep

*Words by Elizabeth Akers Allen (pseud. Florence Percy) • Music by William Martin • 1860*

The "Literaries," evening get-togethers of the Literary Society, were started in De Smet to give everybody a good time. There was a different program every Friday, and anyone who could help pitched in.

*At the musical evening Laura could hardly bear the sadness of this song. All the women were wiping their eyes, and the men were clearing their throats.*    LTP, *page 223*

**With a gentle lilt**

1. Back - ward, turn back - ward, Oh Time in thy flight,
2. O - ver my heart__ in days that are flown,

Make me a child a - gain just for to - night. Moth - er, come back from the
No love like moth - er love ev - er was shown; No oth - er wor - ship a -

ech - o - less shore, Take me a - gain to your heart as of yore;
bides and en - dures, Faith - ful, un - self - ish, and pa - tient like yours;

Kiss from my fore-head the fur-rows of care,
None like a moth-er can charm a-way pain

Smooth the few
From the sick

sil - ver threads out of my hair,
soul and the world - wea - ry brain.

O - ver my slum - bers your
Slum - ber's soft calm o'er my

lov - ing watch keep;
heav - y lids creep;

Rock me to sleep, moth-er, rock me to sleep!
Rock me to sleep, moth-er, rock me to sleep!

3. Mother, dear mother, the years have been long
   Since I last hushed to your lullaby song;
   Sing then and unto my soul it shall seem
   Womanhood's years have been only a dream.
   Clasped to your heart in a loving embrace,
   With your light lashes just sweeping my face,
   Never hereafter to wake or to weep;
   Rock me to sleep, mother, rock me to sleep!

# Love's Old Sweet Song

*Words by Clifton Bingham • Music by James L. Molloy • 1884*

James Lyman Molloy, an Irish lawyer, was also well known as a composer. This is the most famous of his songs.

*The evening before Laura's wedding Pa played all the old tunes that she had known ever since she could remember and finished with "Just a song at twilight. . . ." HGY, page 277*

Andante con moto

Once in the dear dead days be-yond re-call When on the world the
E-ven to-day we hear love's song of yore, Deep in our hearts it

mists be-gan to fall, Out of the dreams that rose in hap-py throng,
swells for-ev-er-more. Foot-steps may fal-ter, wea-ry grow the way,

go, Though the heart be wea - ry, sad the day and

long, Still to us at twi - light comes love's old

song, Comes love's old sweet song.

# Favorites of Long Ago

# Buy a Broom

*Words Anonymous • Traditional Austrian Tune • Circa 1830*

This nursery favorite was originally popular with adults; an early presentation at the Park Theatre in New York met with "the most Unbounded Approbation." It was a song that Laura loved when she learned it from her Cousin Lena in the railroad camp at Silver Lake.

SSL, *page* 94

Waltz tempo

1. From Teutch - land I___ come with my light wares all la - den To___ dear hap - py___ Eng - land, in sum - mer's gay bloom. Then lis - ten, fair la - dy, and young pret - ty maid - en: Will you buy of___ this___

wan - d'ring Ba - var - ian a broom? Buy a broom, buy a

broom! Will you buy of__ this__ wan - d'ring Ba - var - ian a broom?

2. To brush off the insects that come to annoy you
   You'll find it quite useful by night and by day,
   And what better exercise, pray, can employ you,
   Than to sweep all vexatious intruders away?
       Buy a broom, buy a broom!
       Than to sweep all vexatious intruders away?

3. Ere winter comes on for sweet home soon departing
   My toils for your favor again I'll resume,
   And while gratitude's tear in my eyelid is starting,
   Bless the time that in England I cried buy a broom!
       Buy a broom, buy a broom!
       Bless the time that in England I cried buy a broom!

# Camptown Races

*Words and Music by Stephen Foster • 1850*

Many of Stephen Foster's melodies are reminiscent of African-American folk
music; the chorus of "Camptown Races" is similar to "Roll, Jordan, Roll."
*The music would go rollicking while Pa and Mr. Boast sang: "I bet my money on the
bob-tailed mare!" Ma did not approve of gambling, but her toe could not stop tapping to
this tune.*

SSL, *page 212*

1. The Camp-town la-dies sing this song, Doo-dah! doo-dah! The
2. The long-tail fil-ly and the big black horse, Doo-dah! doo-dah! They

Camp-town race-track five miles long, Oh! doo-dah-day! I
fly the track and they both cut a-cross, Oh! doo-dah-day! The

come down there with my hat caved in, Doo-dah! doo-dah! I
blind horse sticking in a big mud hole, Doo-dah! doo-dah!

go back home with a pock-et full of tin, Oh! doo-dah - day!
Can't touch bot-tom with a ten - foot pole, Oh! doo-dah - day!

**Chorus**

Goin' to run all night! Goin' to run all day! I

bet my mon-ey on the bob-tailed mare And you bet yours on the gray!

3. Old muley cow come onto the track, Doo-dah! doo-dah!
   The bobtail fling her over her back, Oh! doo-dah-day!
   Then fly along like a railroad car, Doo-dah! doo-dah!
   Running a race with a shooting star, Oh! doo-dah-day!

   (Chorus)

4. See them flying on a ten-mile heat, Doo-dah! doo-dah!
   Round the racetrack, then repeat, Oh! doo-dah-day!
   I win my money on the bobtailed mare, Doo-dah! doo-dah!
   I keep my money in an old tow bag, Oh! doo-dah-day!

   (Chorus)

# Golden Years Are Passing By

*Words and Music by Will L. Thompson • 1879*

Will L. Thompson was a prolific nineteenth-century song writer whose sentimental ballads enjoyed great popularity.

*The family sat in the deepening dusk. The land flattened to blackness, and in the clear air above it the stars hung low. Then Pa said: "Here is one for you girls." Softly he sang: the music floated away and was gone.*

HGY, *page 156*

**Meditative**

1. Gold - en years are pass - ing by,— Hap - py, hap - py gold-en years, Pass - ing on the wings of time, These hap - py gold - en years. Call them back as they go by, Sweet their mem - 'ries

2. Gold - en years are pass - ing by,— Pre - cious, pre - cious gold-en years, Let no i - dle hour be spent, With sor - row, grief, and tears. Ah! The good we all may do, As the mo - ments

are,— Oh, im-prove them as they fly, These hap-py gold-en years.
pass,— To your no-bler self be true, Re-ward will come at last.

**Chorus**

Gold-en years, gold-en years, Hap-py gold-en years,—

Oh, im-prove them as they fly, These hap-py gold-en years.

3. Golden years are passing by,
   Fleeting, fleeting swiftly on,
   Life is but a passing hour,
   Before we know 'tis gone;
   Soon the parting time will come,
   Day by day it nears.
   Have you done your duty well,
   These happy golden years?

   (Chorus)

# Paddle Your Own Canoe

*Words and Music by Harry Clifton • 1867*

This is one of the moralizing songs, based on homely maxims, that were highly esteemed during the late nineteenth century.

*Comfortably settled in at Silver Lake's deserted railroad camp forty miles away from the nearest neighbors, Pa said: "Now here's something worth singing. That's what we'll be doing this winter."*  SSL, *page 148*

1. I've trav - eled a - bout a bit in my time, And of trou - bles I've seen a
2. It's all ver - y well to de - pend on a friend, That is if you've proved him

few; _____ But found it bet - ter in ev - 'ry clime To
true, _____ But you'll find it bet - ter by far in the end To

world you go trav - el - ing through,_____ And nev - er sit down, with a

tear or a frown, But pad - dle your own ca - noe._____

3. If a hurricane rise in the midday skies,
   And the sun is lost to view;
   Move steadily by with a steadfast eye,
   And paddle your own canoe;
   The daisies that grow in the bright green fields
   Are blooming so sweet for you,
   So never sit down, with a tear or a frown,
   But paddle your own canoe.

   (Chorus)

# It Will Never Do to Give It Up So

*Words and Music by Daniel Decatur Emmett • 1843*

This was one of Daniel Emmett's early minstrel successes. The chorus shows the influence of Irish and Scottish reels.

*During one of the long winter's savage blizzards when Pa's hands were too cracked and stiff to play the fiddle, he led the family in singing this spirited ditty about facing up to trouble on "the old Jim River."*          LW, *page 290*

1. I'm old Mis-ter Brown just from the South, I
2. The old Jim Riv-er I float-ed down, I

left Lynch - burg in the time of the drouth; The times they got so
ran my boat up - on the groun'; The drift log come with a

bad in the place That we poor folks dared not show our__ face.
rush - ing din And stove both ends of my old boat__ in.

**Chorus**

It will nev - er do to give it up so, It will

nev - er do to give it up so, It will nev - er do to give it up so, Mis - ter Brown, It will nev - er do to give it up so.

3. The old log rake me aft and fore,
   It left my cookhouse on the shore;
   I thought it wouldn't do to give it up so
   So I scull myself ashore with the old banjo.

   (Chorus)

4. I gets on shore and feels very glad,
   I looks at the banjo and feels very mad;
   I walks up the bank that's slick as glass,
   Up went my heels and I light upon the grass.

   (Chorus)

5. By golly, but it surely made me laugh,
   With my boat I made a raft;
   I had a pine tree for a sail
   And steered her down with my coattail.

   (Chorus)

6. That same night as the sun did set,
   I 'rived in town with my clothes all wet;
   Then I built up a great big fire,
   If that's not true then I am a liar.

   (Chorus)

# Oh, Susanna

*Words Traditional USA, California Gold Rush Version • Music by Stephen Foster • 1848*

This parody of Stephen Foster's minstrel ditty was called "The California Immigrant"; it was first heard at the farewell banquet for a young man who was leaving for California on the sailing ship *Eliza*. The new version became the theme song of the forty-niners and later pioneers.

*Pa often sang it beside his prairie campfire.*

LHP, *page* 332

1. I —— came from Sa - lem Cit - y With my
It —— rained all night the day I left, The

wash - pan on my knee, I'm —— going to Cal - i -
weath - er it was dry, The —— sun so hot I

for - ni - a, The gold dust for to see.
froze to death, Oh broth - ers, don't you cry!

Oh Su - san - na, Don't you cry for me! I'm___ going to Cal - i - for - ni - a, With my wash - pan on my knee!

2. I jumped aboard the *'Liza* ship
   And traveled on the sea,
   And every time I thought of home,
   I wished it wasn't me!
   The vessel reared like any horse,
   That had of oats a wealth,
   I found it wouldn't throw me so
   I thought I'd throw myself!

   (Chorus)

3. I thought of all the pleasant times
   We've had together here,
   I thought I ought to cry a bit,
   But couldn't find a tear.
   The pilot's bread* was in my mouth,
   The gold dust in my eye,
   And though I'm going far away,
   Dear brothers, don't you cry!

   (Chorus)

4. I soon shall be in Frisco
   And there I'll look around,
   And when I see the gold lumps there,
   I'll pick them off the ground.
   I'll scrape the mountains clean, my boys,
   I'll drain the rivers dry,
   A pocketful of rocks bring home,
   So brothers, don't you cry!

   (Chorus)

   *(hard tack)

# The Campbells Are Coming

*Words and Music Traditional Scottish • Circa 1715*

*The evening before starting his three-hundred-mile walk to get work, Pa played for a long time in the twilight. This stirring march was one of the tunes. When bedtime came, he said: "Take good care of the old fiddle, Caroline. It puts heart into a man."*  BPC, *page 211*

**Verse**

1. Up - on the Lo - monds I lay, I lay, Up -
on the Lo - monds I lay, I lay; I look - ed down to
bon - nie Loch Lev - en, And heard the bon - nie pi - brochs play.

2. The great Ar - gyle, he goes be - fore; He
makes his can - nons loud - ly roar; Wi' sound o' trum - pet,
pipe, and drum, The Camp - bells are com - ing, Hur - rah! Hur - rah!

*D. C. al Fine*

3. The Campbells they are a' in arms;
   Their loyal faith and truth to show;
   Wi' banners rattling in the wind,
   The Campbells are coming, Hurrah! Hurrah!

(Chorus)

49

# All the Blue Bonnets Are over the Border

*Words by Sir Walter Scott • Traditional Scottish Tune • Circa 1820*

The "Border Ballad" from Scott's *Monastery*, set to an ancient Scottish air, became widely popular in the United States during the early nineteenth century. Its rousing strains helped to ease the rigors of the long winter.

*Pa said: "Blamed if that old tune don't give me the spunk to like fighting even a blizzard!"*

LW, page 44

**Verse**

1. Man-y a ban-ner spread, flut-ters a-bove your head,
2. Come from the hills where your hir-sels are graz-ing,

Man-y a crest that is fa-mous in sto-ry: Mount, and make read-y then,
Come from the glen of the buck and the roe;___ Come to the crag where the

sons of the moun-tain glen, Fight! for your homes and the old Scot-tish glo-ry!
bea-con is blaz-ing, Come with the buck-ler, the lance, and the bow.___

*D. C. al Fine*

3. Trumpets are sounding, war steeds are bounding,
   Stand to your arms and march in good order;
   England shall many a day tell of the bloody fray,
   When the blue bonnets came over the border.

   (Chorus)

# Where There's a Will There's a Way

*Words and Music by Harry Clifton • 1867*

*The hard winter was over; the train had come at last with food. The Ingalls family and their friends the Boasts celebrated springtime by having the Christmas dinner they had all gone without. Afterward everyone joined in this new song, and as they sang, fear and suffering seemed to rise like a dark cloud and float away on the music.*    LW, *page 333*

1. This life is a dif - fi - cult rid -
2. Did you nev - er hear tell of the spi -
3. Do you think that by sit - ting and sigh -

dle    For how man - y peo - ple we see _____ With
der    That tried up the wall hard to climb? _____ If
ing    You'll ev - er ob - tain all you want? _____ It's

faces as long as a fid - dle That ought to be
not, just take that as a guid - er, You'll find it will
cowards a - lone that are cry - ing And fool - ish - ly

shin - ing with glee. _____ I am sure in this world there are
serve you in time. _____ Nine times it tried hard to be
say - ing "I can't!" _____ It's on - ly by plod - ding and

plen - ty Of _ good things e - nough for us all. _____
mount - ing And ev - 'ry time it stuck fast. _____
striv - ing And la - bor - ing up the steep hill, _____

_ And _ yet there's not one out of twen -
_ But it tried hard a - gain with - out count -
_ Of life that you'll ev - er be thriv -

ty, But___ thinks that his share is too small.___
ing, And of course it suc - ceed - ed at last.___
ing, Which you'll do if you've on - ly the will.___

**Chorus**

Then what is the use of re - pin - ing For where there's a

will there's a way,_____ And to - mor - row the sun may be

shin - ing Al - though it is cloud-y to - day._____

# BALLADS, GAMES, AND DANCES

# Billy Boy

*Words and Music Traditional USA*

This folk song is a nonsense version of the grim classic ballad "Lord Randal."
*The happy winter evenings had begun at Silver Lake. Gaily, Pa played and sang: "She
can make a cherry pie, charming Billy." His eyes twinkled at Ma while the music laughed
and whirled.* SSL, *page 211*

**Moderately, brightly**

1. Oh, where have you been, Bil - ly
2. Did she bid you to come in, Bil - ly

boy, Bil - ly boy; Oh, where have you
boy, Bil - ly boy; Did she bid you to come

been, charm - ing Bil - ly? I have been to seek a
in, charm - ing Bil - ly? Yes, she bade me to come

wife; She's the joy_____ of my life, But she's a
in; There's a dim - ple in her chin, But she's a

young thing and can - not leave her moth - er. _____
young thing and can - not leave her moth - er. _____

3. Did she set for you a chair, Billy boy, Billy boy;
   Did she set for you a chair, charming Billy?
   Yes, she set for me a chair;
   She has ringlets in her hair,
   But she's a young thing and cannot leave her mother.

4. Can she make a cherry pie, Billy boy, Billy boy;
   Can she make a cherry pie, charming Billy?
   She can make a cherry pie,
   With a twinkle in her eye,
   But she's a young thing and cannot leave her mother.

5. Is she often seen at church, Billy boy, Billy boy;
   Is she often seen at church, charming Billy?
   Yes, she's often seen at church,
   With a bonnet white as birch,
   But she's a young thing and cannot leave her mother.

6. How tall is she, Billy boy, Billy boy;
   How tall is she, charming Billy?
   She's as tall as any pine,
   And as straight as a pumpkin vine,
   But she's a young thing and cannot leave her mother.

7. Are her eyes very bright, Billy boy, Billy boy;
   Are her eyes very bright, charming Billy?
   Yes, her eyes are very bright,
   But, alas, they're minus sight,
   But she's a young thing and cannot leave her mother.

8. How old is she, Billy boy, Billy boy;
   How old is she, charming Billy?
   She is four times seven,
   Twenty-eight and eleven,
   But she's a young thing and cannot leave her mother.

# Buffalo Gals

*Words and Music by John Hodges (pseud. Cool White) • 1848*

Originally called "Lubly Fan," this minstrel-show number and play-party song underwent various changes of name to fit different localities.

*When the fiddle sang it at Grandpa's dance and Pa called "Swing your partners," skirts swirled and boots stamped and partners bowed and separated and met and bowed again.*

LHBW, *page 145*

1. As I went lum-b'ring down the street,
2. I ax'd her if she'd have some talk,
3. I'd like to make that gal my wife,

Down the street, down the street, A love-ly gal I
Have some talk, have some talk, Her feet cov-ered up the
Gal my wife, gal my wife, I would be hap-py

chanced to meet, Oh! She was fair to view.
whole side-walk As she stood close by me.
all my life If I had her by my side.

**Chorus**

Oh, you Buf-fa-lo gals, will you come out to-night, Will you
come out to-night, will you come out to-night, Buf-fa-lo gals, will you
come out to-night, To dance by the light of the moon?

# The Singing School

*Words and Music by P. Benson • 1869*

Gently satirized in this nonsense song, the singing school was a long-established part of American musical tradition.

*Laura loved the singing school and its gay evenings. First the class learned the notes; then they practiced scales, exercises, and songs. At recess everyone talked and laughed together. And on the way home with Almanzo, Laura sang this song again.* HGY, *page 212*

With humor

1. Oh, child-hood's joys are ver - y great, A - swing-in' on his moth - er's gate, A - eat - in' can - dy till his mouth Is all stuck up from north to south, And oth - er things he

2. And it's con - sid - ered ver - y nice, To skate up - on the friz up ice, Un - less you chance to fall ker - whack! And there - by cause your head to crack. And when you go from

likes quite well, That___ I ain't time just here to tell, But
home to dine, A___ roast - ed tur - key's ver - y fine, But

though I have to mind the rule, I'd rath - er go to sing - ing school!
still I think it's more joy - ful, To go - o - o to sing - ing school.

**Chorus**

Oh, the sing - ing school's beau - ti - ful, Oh, the

sing - ing school's beau - ti - ful, If you'll have me for your teach - er, I shall be a hap-py crea-ture For I dote up-on the sing-ing school. The

sing-ing -ing -ing -ing -ing -ing -ing, Sing-ing -ing -ing -ing -ing -ing -ing,

Sing-ing -ing -ing -ing -ing -ing -ing, Sing-ing -ing -ing -ing -ing -ing -ing school.

3. Some think that nothin's half so good,
As oysters roasted, fried, or stewed,
And others think the pleasure's more
A-slidin' on a cellar door.
So some think this and some think that,
But all agree there's greater sat-
Isfaction to be always had,
At singing school as I have said.

(Chorus)

4. Oh, sweet the breath of dewy morn,
A-blowin' sadly through the corn,
While golden rays of mystic light
Is heard upon the dawn of night.
But superfine, ecstatic bliss,
You'll always find and never miss,
If you will only mind this rule,
And always go to singing school.

(Chorus)

# Captain Jinks

*Words by William Horace Lingard • Music by T. Maclagan • 1869*

This is an English music-hall number that was an instant success when introduced in the United States. The "horse" referred to is not a four-legged one but the troop of marines for whose rations their captain was responsible.

*Ma set a pan of beautiful brown baked beans and a pan of golden corn-bread on the table.*
*Then Pa sang: "I'm Captain Jinks. . . ."*

BPC, *page* 338

With bouncy humor

1. I'm__ Cap - tain Jinks of the Horse Ma - rines, I
2. I__ joined my corps when twen - ty - one, Of

of - ten go be - yond my means, To__ court the girls all
course I thought it cap - i - tal fun, When the en - e - my came then

feed my horse on corn and beans, Al - though 'tis far be -

yond my means, For I'm cap - tain in the ar - my.

3. The first day I went out to drill,
   The bugle sound made me quite ill,
   At the balance step my hat it fell,
   And that wouldn't do for the army.
   The officers they all did shout,
   They all did shout, they all did shout,
   The officers they all did shout,
   "Oh, that's the curse of the army."

   (Chorus)

4. My tailor's bills came in so fast,
   Forced me one to day leave at last,
   And ladies too no more did cast
   Sheep's eyes at me in the army.
   My creditors at me did shout,
   At me did shout, at me did shout,
   My creditors at me did shout,
   "Why, kick him out of the army."

   (Chorus)

# Old Dan Tucker

*Words and Music by Daniel Decatur Emmett • 1843*

A robust ballad with many stanzas that has become known as a traditional American song. The tune is often used for folk dancing.

*Mr. Edwards, the family friend, danced to the fiddle's music like a jumping jack in the moonlight. When it was time to go home, Pa played him down the road with "Old Dan Tucker."*

LHP, *page 69*

Lively, with humor

1. Old Dan Tuck-er was a fine old man, He washed his face in the fry-ing pan, He combed his hair with a wag-on wheel And died of the tooth-ache in his heel.

2. Old Dan Tuck - er went to town, Rid-ing a mule and lead-ing a houn'; Houn' barked and the mule jumped, Threw old Dan right o-ver a stump.

66

Git out the way for old Dan Tuck-er! He's too late to git his sup-per,

Sup-per's o - ver and dish-es washed, Noth-ing left but a piece of squash!

3. I come to town the other night,
   I hear the noise and saw the fight;
   The watchman was arunnin' roun'
   Crying, "Old Dan Tucker's come to town."

   (Chorus)

4. Old Dan he went down to the mill
   To get some meal to put in the swill;
   The miller swore by the point of his knife
   He never see'd such a man in his life.

   (Chorus)

5. Tucker is a nice old man,
   He used to ride our darby ram;
   He sent him whizzin' down the hill,
   If he hadn't got up, he'd lay there still.

   (Chorus)

6. Old Dan begun in early life
   To play the banjo and the fife;
   He play the children all to sleep,
   And then into his bunk he creep.

   (Chorus)

# Old Grimes

*Words adapted from "Old Grimes" by Albert Gorton Greene • Tune: "Auld Lang Syne"*
*• Circa 1873*

*Pa sang his own version of Greene's song while Ma was making cheese. He thought Old Grimes might have staggered along if his wife hadn't skimmed off every bit of cream. But "She was a mean, tight-fisted woman. Old Grimes got so thin the wind blew him away," Pa said.*

LHBW, *page 192*

**Slow, with mock sadness**

Old Grimes is dead, that good old man, We ne'er shall see him more, He used to wear an old grey coat, All but-toned down be-fore. Old Grimes's wife made skim - milk cheese, Old Grimes he drank the whey, There

came an east wind from the west And blew Old Grimes a - way.

# Polly-Wolly-Doodle

*Words and Music Traditional USA*

An exuberant bit of foolery, this song is believed to be of African-American origin. It has become a favorite of college glee clubs.

*When Pa had agreed that he and Laura could buy an organ for Mary, he said: "By jinks! I feel like celebrating. Bring me my fiddle, Half-Pint, and we'll have a little music."*

HGY, *page* 155

**Chorus**

Fare - well, fare - well, Fare - well, my fai - ry fay, For I'm off to Louis - i - a - na For to see my Su - sy An - na, Sing - ing pol - ly - wol - ly - doo - dle all the day.

3. Oh, a grasshopper sittin' on a railroad track,
   Sing polly-wolly-doodle all the day;
   A-pickin' his teeth with a carpet tack,
   Sing polly-wolly-doodle all the day.

   (Chorus)

4. Oh, I went to bed but it wasn't no use,
   Sing polly-wolly-doodle all the day;
   My feet stuck out for a chicken roost,
   Sing polly-wolly-doodle all the day.

   (Chorus)

5. Behind the barn, down on my knees,
   Sing polly-wolly-doodle all the day;
   I thought I heard that chicken sneeze,
   Sing polly-wolly-doodle all the day.

   (Chorus)

6. He sneezed so hard with the whoopin' cough,
   Sing polly-wolly-doodle all the day;
   He sneezed his head and his tail right off,
   Sing polly-wolly-doodle all the day.

   (Chorus)

# Pop! Goes the Weasel

*Words and Music Traditional USA*

A standard tune at country dances, this song goes back to Old English sources.
*Once Pa said to Laura and Mary, "Watch, and maybe you can see the weasel pop out this*
*time." "Pop!" said his finger on the string; "Goes the weasel!" sang the fiddle. But Laura*
*and Mary hadn't seen Pa's finger make the string pop. He was so quick they could never*
*catch him.* LHBW, *page 98*

wea - sel! All a - round the cob - bler's bench, The
mon - key chased the wea - sel, The preach - er kissed the
cob - bler's wife —— Pop! goes the wea - sel!

# Uncle John (*A Singing Game*)

*Words Traditional USA • Tune: "Yankee Doodle"*

This singing game is a love story. It may have been derived from the medieval
song in which an imprisoned knight is saved from death by the daughter of a king
who keeps him in confinement.

*At Laura's first school the little girls always played ring-around-a-rosy at recess till one
day she said: "Let's play Uncle John!"*                          BPC, *page* 158

Not too fast

1. Un - cle John is sick a - bed, What shall we
send him? A piece of pie, a piece of cake, A piece of ap - ple
dump - ling.

What shall we send it in?
Who shall we send it by?

In a piece of pa - per. Pa - per is not
By the gov - er - nor's daugh - ter. Take her by the

fine e - nough; ___ In a gold - en sau - cer.
lil - y - white hand, And lead her o'er the wa - ter.

2. _____ so they say,
Goes acourting night and day,
Sword and pistol by his side,
And _____ to be his bride.
Takes her by the lily-white hand,
And leads her o'er the water,
Here's a kiss, and there's a kiss,
For Mr. _____'s daughter.

*DIRECTIONS:*
   *1. The players circle and sing the first verse.*
   *2. At the words "governor's daughter" all fall down.*
   *3. The last one down stands apart and whispers to a*
      *friend the name of a favorite person and then returns*
      *to the ring and stands in the center.*
   *4. The friend announces the name, and the players circle*
      *again, singing the second verse with the names of the*
      *couple inserted at the proper places.*
   *5. At the end, the ring breaks up. Everyone dances around,*
      *clapping hands.*

# Weevily Wheat

*Words and Music Traditional USA*

There are memories of the Jacobite uprising of 1745 and of Bonnie Prince
Charlie in this dance song. It was widely used at play-parties with the steps of
the Virginia Reel.
*When Pa was safe at home after being snowed in at Plum Creek, he said: "Laura, if you'll
bring me the fiddle-box, I'll play you a tune." Then he filled the house with this jaunty
music.*

BPC, *page 336*

1. Oh, Char - ley he's a fine young man, Oh,
2. Char - ley's here and Char - ley's there And

Char - ley he's a dan - dy! Char - ley likes to
Char - ley's o - ver the o - cean, Char - ley he'll come

kiss the girls And he can do it han - dy!
back some day Un - less he takes a no - tion.

I don't want none of your weev - i - ly wheat,

I don't want none of your bar - ley, I want fine flour in

half an hour, To bake a cake for Char - ley!

3. Coffee grows on white-oak trees,
   River flows with brandy,
   Choose you one to roam with you
   Sweet as 'lasses candy.

   (Chorus)

# PATRIOTIC SONGS

# The Star-Spangled Banner

*Words by Francis Scott Key • Music by John Stafford Smith • 1814*

The words of our national anthem were written during the bombardment of Fort McHenry, near Baltimore, during the War of 1812. They were set to "Anacreon in Heaven," an English melody.

*At the Fourth of July celebration when Almanzo was a little boy, the band played and everybody sang: "Oh, say, can you see . . ."*　　　　FB, *page 178*

1. Oh — say, can you see, by the dawn's ear - ly light, What so proud - ly we hailed at the twi-light's last gleam - ing? Whose broad stripes and bright stars, through the per - il - ous fight, O'er the ram - parts we watched were so

2. On the shore dim - ly seen through the mists of the deep Where the foe's haugh - ty host in dread si - lence re - pos - es, What is that which the breeze, o'er the tow - er - ing steep As it fit - ful - ly blows, half con-

3. Oh — thus be it ev - er, when — free men shall stand Be - tween their loved home and the war's des - o - la - tion! Bless'd with vic-to - ry and peace, may the heav-en-res - cued land Praise the Power that hath made and pre-

# When Johnny Comes Marching Home

*Words and Music by Patrick Gilmore (pseud. Louis Lambert) • 1863*

Patrick Gilmore, a famous bandmaster, published this song under the pseudo-
nym Louis Lambert. It has been a favorite ever since the Civil War.
*The night of Pa's return from working as a harvester, he looked round at
Ma and the girls and said: "I have missed this." Then he began to play songs
of home.*

*BPC, page 244*

1. When John - ny comes march - ing home a - gain, Hur - rah, \_\_\_\_ hur -
2. The old church bell will peal with joy, Hur - rah, \_\_\_\_ hur -
3. Get read - y for the jub - i - lee, Hur - rah, \_\_\_\_ hur -

rah, \_\_\_\_ We'll give him a heart - y wel - come then, Hur -
rah, \_\_\_\_ To wel - come home our dar - ling boy, Hur -
rah, \_\_\_\_ We'll give the he - ro three times three, Hur -

# Hail Columbia

*Words by Joseph Hopkinson • Music by Philip Phile • 1798*

This song was written at a time when war with France was thought to be inevitable. For many years it rivaled "The Star-Spangled Banner" as one of our great patriotic songs.

*After supper the Ingalls family all gathered in the warmth of the stove, and Pa sang: "Hail Columbia, happy land!"*

SSL, *page* 154

**Majestic march tempo**

1. Hail! Co-lum - bia, hap - py land! Hail! ye he - roes,
2. Im - mor - tal pa - triots, rise once more! De - fend your rights, de -

heav'n-born band! Who fought and bled in Free - dom's_ cause,
fend your shore! Let no rude foe, with im - pious_ hand,

Who fought and bled in Free - dom's_ cause, And when the storm of
Let no rude foe, with im - pious_ hand, In - vade the shrine where

## Chorus

Firm, u-ni-ted, let us be, Ral-ly-ing round our lib-er-ty;

As a band of broth-ers join'd, Peace and safe-ty we shall find.

3. Sound, sound the trump of fame!
   Let Washington's great name
   Ring through the world with loud applause!
   Ring through the world with loud applause!
   Let ev'ry clime to freedom dear,
   Listen with a joyful ear!
   With equal skill, with godlike power,
   He governs in the fearful hour
   Of horrid war, or guides with ease
   The happier times of honest peace.

   (Chorus)

4. Behold the chief who now commands!
   Once more to serve his country stands!
   The rock on which the storm will beat,
   The rock on which the storm will beat,
   But arm'd in virtue firm and true,
   His hopes are fix'd on Heaven and you;
   When hope was sinking in dismay,
   When glooms obscured Columbia's day;
   His steady mind, from changes free,
   Resolved on death or liberty!

   (Chorus)

# Uncle Sam's Farm

*Words and Music by Jesse Hutchinson, Jr. • Original music arranged by N. Barker • 1850*

Concert tours of singing families were a popular form of musical entertainment in the United States from 1840 to 1860. Best known were the Hutchinsons. Jesse Hutchinson, Jr., wrote a number of their songs.

*Pa sang this song often as he drove westward to the Dakota Territory. Even baby Grace joined in, though she didn't bother to follow the tune.*　　SSL, *page 62*

1. Of ___ all the might - y na - tions In the east or in the west, Oh, this glo - rious Yan - kee na - tion Is the great - est and the best, We have
2. St. ___ Law - rence marks our north - ern line As fast her wa - ters flow; And the Ri - o Grande our south - ern bound, 'Way down to Mex - i - co; From the

room for all cre - a - tion And our ban - ner is un-furl'd, Here's a
great At - lan - tic O - cean Where the sun be - gins to dawn, Leap a -

gen - 'ral in - vi - ta - tion To the peo - ple of the world.
cross the Rock - y Moun - tains Far a - way to O - re - gon.

**Chorus**

Oh, come a - way! Come a - way!

Come a-way, I say! Oh, come a-way! Come a-way! Come right a-way! Oh,___ come to this coun-try and    have no fear of harm, Our_ Un-cle Sam is rich e-nough To

give us all  a farm!

3. While the South shall raise the cotton
   And the West the corn and pork,
   New England manufactories
   Shall do up the finer work,
   For the deep and flowing waterfalls
   That course along our hills,
   Are just the thing for washing sheep
   And driving cotton mills.

   (Chorus)

4. Our fathers gave us Liberty
   But little did they dream,
   The grand results that pour along
   This mighty age of steam,
   For our mountains, lakes, and rivers
   Are all a blaze of fire,
   And we send news by lightning
   On the telegraphic wire.

   (Chorus)

5. Yes! we're bound to beat the nations
   For our motto's "Go ahead,"
   And we'll tell the foreign countries
   That our people are well-fed,
   For the nations must remember
   That Uncle Sam is not a fool,
   For the people do the voting
   And the children go to school.

   (Chorus)

# America

*Words by Reverend Samuel Francis Smith • Traditional English Tune • 1831*

The words to this song were written at the request of Lowell Mason, the "father
of public-school music in the United States." They were first sung at a children's
celebration of Independence Day in Boston.

*When Laura heard them, her whole mind seemed to be lighted up by their message of free-*
*dom under Divine Law.*                                        LTP, *page 75*

3. Let music swell the breeze,
   And ring from all the trees
   Sweet freedom's song;
   Let mortal tongues awake;
   Let all that breathe partake;
   Let rocks their silence break
   The sound prolong.

4. Our father's God to Thee,
   Author of liberty,
   To Thee we sing;
   Long may our land be bright
   With freedom's holy light;
   Protect us by Thy might,
   Great God, our King!

# Love and Courtship

# The Blue Juniata

*Words and Music by Mrs. Marion Dix Sullivan • 1844*

*Although the Juniata is a little river in Pennsylvania, Ma sang this highly romanticized ballad out on the prairie. When Laura asked her where the voice of Alfarata went, Ma answered, "Oh, I do suppose she went west. That's what Indians do." Then Pa explained how the government was moving the Indians westward and how the settlers were taking over their land.*

LHP, *page 234*

**With motion and strong beat**

1. Wild roved an In - dian maid, Bright Al - fa -
2. "Bold is my war - rior good, The love of Al - fa -
3. So sang the In - dian maid, Bright Al - fa -

ra - ta, Where flow the wa - ters Of the
ra - ta, Proud wave his sun - ny plumes A -
ra - ta, Where sweep the wa - ters Of the

blue —— Ju – ni – a – ta.
long the Ju – ni – a – ta.
blue —— Ju – ni – a – ta.

Strong and true my
Soft and low he
Fleet - ing years have

ar - rows are, And In my paint - ed quiv - er,
speaks to me, And then his war - cry sound - ing,
borne a - way The voice of Al - fa - ra - ta,

Swift goes my light ca - noe A - down the rap - id riv - er.
Rings his voice in thun - der loud From height to height re - sound - ing."
Still flow the wa - ters Of the blue —— Ju - ni - a - ta.

# Come In and Shut the Door

*Words by J. P. H. • Music by J. G. Callcott • 1863*

*One snowy Christmas Eve Laura missed Almanzo, who was visiting his old home far
away. He might forget her, she thought, or wish that he had not given her a ring. . . .
Someone knocked at the door. When Laura opened it, she could not believe her eyes, for
there stood Almanzo himself. "Come in!" Pa called. "Come in and shut the door!"*

HGY, *page 227*

1. Oh,— do not stand so long out-side, Why need you be so shy! The— peo-ple's ears are
2. Nay— do not say "No, thank you, Jane," With such a bash-ful smile; You— said when la - dies
3. You— say I did not an - swer you, To what you said last night; I — heard your ques - tion

o - pen, John, As they are pass - ing by! You can - not tell what
whis - pered "No," They meant "Yes" all the while! My fa - ther too will
in the dark, Thought on it in the light; And now my lips shall

they may think, They've said strange things be - fore; _____ And if you wish to
wel - come you, I told you that be - fore; _____ It don't look well to
ut - ter what My heart has said be - fore, _____ Yes, dear - est, I... but

talk a - while, Come in and shut the door.
stand out here, Come in and shut the door. Come in, come
wait a - while, Come in and shut the door.

in, come in, come in, come in, come in, Come in and shut the door.

95

# Green Grows the Laurel

*Words and Music Traditional USA*

A very old song of lovers' parting and reunion. The words "orange and blue" refer to William of Orange. In the United States they were sometimes changed to "red, white, and blue."

*Out on the prairie Pa sang this to Ma when he was leaving for an overnight trip to town.*

LHP, *page* 207

1. I once had a sweet heart, but now I've got none, She's gone and she's left me to weep and to moan; She's gone and she's left me, but con- tent- ed I'll be, For I'll get an- oth- er one bet- ter than she.

2. She wrote me a let- ter, four red ros- y lines, She wrote me an- oth- er all twist- ed in twines; ___ Keep your love let- ter and I will keep mine, And write to your sweet-heart and I'll write to mine.

**Chorus**

So green grows the lau-rel, and so does the rue, So woe-ful, my love, at the part-ing with you. But by our next meet-ing our love we'll re-new; We'll change the green lau-rel to the or-ange and blue.

3. She passes my window both early and late,
   And the looks that she gives me, they make my heart break,
   And the looks that she gives me a thousand times o'er,
   "You are the sweetheart I once did adore."

   (Chorus)

4. I ofttimes do wonder why young maids love men,
   I ofttimes do wonder why young men love them;
   But by my experience, I now ought to know
   Young maids are deceivers wherever they go.

   (Chorus)

# In Dreamland Far Away

*Words by George Birdseye • Music by Hart Pease Danks • 1887*

George Birdseye was a New York journalist and a friend of Stephen Foster. Hart Pease Danks is the composer of "Silver Threads Among the Gold."
*Lamplight shone from the windows of the little prairie house. Pa was playing the fiddle; his voice rose with the music of this song, one that he often sang to Ma.* HGY, *page 216*

1. A beau - ti - ful cas - tle I've built for thee, In
2. No sor - row shall en - ter our cas - tle walls, For

dream - land far a - way, _____ And there, gen - tle dar - ling, come
joy shall guard the door; _____ No word shall be spo - ken that

**C · G · D7 · G · D7**

dwell with me, Where love — a - lone — has sway. ___ Oh, sweet will be our
e'er re-calls The cares — we knew — be - fore. ___

**G · D dim · D7**

bliss - es, Oh, rare — will be ___ our bliss - es! We'll

**G · C · G · D7 · G**

tell ___ our time by the lov - ers' chime, That strikes — the hour — with kiss - es.

3. Then let us enjoy ev'ry blissful hour!
   Too soon our dreams will break;
   Alas, that we never may have the pow'r
   To live them when we wake!

   (Chorus)

# In the Starlight

*Words by J. E. Carpenter • Music by Stephen Glover • 1843*

J. E. Carpenter and Stephen Glover wrote a number of songs together. This
charming piece has been included in many collections.

*As Almanzo and Laura were driving back from singing school, he said: "I don't know
when I ever saw the stars so bright." Softly, Laura began to sing the starlight song.*

HGY, *page 207*

1. In the star-light, in the star-light, Let us wan-der__ gay__ and__ free, For there's noth-ing in the day-light Half so
2. In the star-light, in the star-light, At the day-light's dew-y__ close, When the night-in-gale is sing-ing His last

# Whip-Poor-Will's Song

*Words and Music by Harrison Millard • 1865*

*Pa said, "I want to try a song I heard a fellow singing the other day. He whistled the chorus. I believe the fiddle will beat his whistling." Pa sang, low and longingly, and "Whip-poor-will" the fiddle answered, fluting and throbbing like the throat of the bird.*

LTP, *page* 135

1. Oh,
2. 'Tis

meet me when day-light is fad - ing, And is dark - en - ing in - to the
said that what - ev - er sweet feel - ings May be throb - bing with - in a fond

night, When song-birds are sing - ing their ves - pers, And the
heart, When list-'ning to whip-poor-will's sing - ing, For a

day has far van-ished from sight; And then I will tell to you,
twelve-month will nev - er de - part; So then we will meet in the

dar - ling, All the love I have cher-ished so long, If
wood -land, Far a - way from the hur - ry - ing throng, And

you will but meet me at eve - ning, When you hear the first whip-poor-will's
whis-per our love to each oth - er, When we hear the first whip-poor-will's

## Chorus

song. _____ Whip-poor-will! Whip-poor-will! You
song. _____

hear the first whip-poor-will's song; Then meet me, oh,

meet me, When you hear the first whip-poor-will's song. _____

3. And in the long years of the future,
   Though our duties may part us awhile,
   And on the return of this evening,
   We'll be severed by many a mile;
   Yet deep in our bosoms we'll cherish
   The affection, so fervent and strong,
   We pledged to each other this evening,
   When we heard the first whip-poor-will's song.

   (Chorus)

# Oh, Whistle and I'll Come to You, My Lad!

*Words by Robert Burns • Traditional Scottish Tune • 1799*

Like most of Burns' songs, the words of this song are partly traditional, partly his own, and are set to a folk melody.

*When Laura sang: "Oh, whistle and I'll come to you, my lad," Almanzo asked: "Would you?" "Of course not!" she answered. "That's only a song."* HGY, *page 183*

Lively
Chorus

Oh,— whis-tle and I'll — come to you, my lad, Oh,— whis-tle and I'll— come to you, my lad, Though fa-ther and mith-er and a' should gae mad, Oh,— whis-tle and I'll — come to you, my lad.

# Wait for the Wagon

*Words and Music Anonymous, USA • Circa 1851*

An old favorite that is still heard today, "Wait for the Wagon" has often been para-
phrased and used as a campaign song.

*When Pa began to sing it as the family rode to church, Ma said "Charles" softly to remind*
*him that it was Sunday. Then all together they sang: "There is a happy land. . . ."*

BPC, *page* 180

Merrily, with bounce

1. Will you
2. (Oh,)

come with me, my Phil - lis dear, To yon blue moun - tain
ev - 'ry Sun - day morn - ing____ My wife is at my

free, Where the blos - soms smell the sweet - est, Come
side, A - wait - ing for the wag - on, And

**1.** rove a - long with me. 2. Oh, we'll all take a ride!

**2.**

**Chorus**

Wait for the wag - on, Wait for the wag - on,

Wait for the wag - on, And we'll all take a ride.

*D. C.* | *last time only*

3. Your lips are red as poppies,
   Your hair so slick and neat,
   All braided up with dahlias,
   And hollyhocks so sweet.

4. It's ev'ry Sunday morning,
   When I am by your side,
   We'll jump into the wagon,
   And all take a ride.

   (Chorus)

5. Together on life's journey,
   We'll travel till we stop,
   And if we have no trouble,
   We'll reach the happy top.

6. Then come with me, sweet Phillis,
   My dear, my lovely bride,
   We'll jump into the wagon,
   And all take a ride.

   (Chorus)

# Beware!

*Words by Henry Wadsworth Longfellow • Music by Charles Moulton • 1865*

The original of Longfellow's poem warns against a flirtatious maiden. But when Cousin Lena sang "Beware!" at Silver Lake, it was about a young man who would prove untrue.

*As Laura and Lena climbed into the buggy, the black ponies gave a little squeal and ran. Everything went rushing by too fast to be seen. Lena began to sing, and Laura joined in with all her voice.*

*SSL, page 48*

**Chorus**

Trust her not, she's fool - ing thee; She's

fool - ing thee; _____ Trust her

not, she's fool - ing thee;__ She's fool - ing thee. _____

3. And she has hair of golden hue,
Take care! take care!
And what she says, it is not true,
Beware! beware!

(Chorus)

4. She gives thee a garland woven fair,
Take care! take care!
It is a fool's cap for thee to wear,
Beware! beware!

(Chorus)

# The Girl I Left Behind Me

*Words Traditional USA • Traditional Irish Tune*

This tune was first printed in Dublin in 1810. It is the traditional type of music played by a band when troops are leaving. This western version is also used for square dancing.

*Pa sang it to Ma when he came back from his long trip to the wheatfields where he had been working as a harvester.*

BPC, *page 244*

E | (E) C#m | (B7) G#m

pret - ty lit - tle girl, The girl I left be - hind me, As I
pret - ty lit - tle girl, The girl I left be - hind me, I __

A | E | A | B7 | E

jogged a - long, my mind ran back To the girl I left be - hind me!
thought of the girl, the sweet lit - tle girl, The girl I'd left be - hind me!

3. She wrote ahead to the place I said
   A letter to remind me;
   She says, "I am true; when you get through
   Ride back and you will find me."
   The sweet little girl, the pretty little girl,
   The girl I left behind me,
   She says, "I am true; when you get through
   Ride back and you will find me."

4. If ever I get off the trail,
   And the Indians they don't find me,
   I'll make my way straight back again
   To the girl I left behind me.
   The sweet little girl, the pretty little girl,
   The girl I left behind me,
   I'll make my way straight back again
   To the girl I left behind me!

# The Big Sunflower

*Words and Music by Bobby Newcomb • 1868*

This is the theme song of Billy Emerson, the well-known minstrel.
*This cheerful tune was Pa's "trouble song." He sang it when blizzards turned the windows into a white blur and snow blew through every crack until it had to be shoveled off the beds in the morning.*

SSL, *page 250*

dark dress trimmed in green. Her eyes are bright as
ask her to be mine. But the an-swer I re-
she had shak-en me. She said she real-ly

eve-ning stars, So lov-ing and so shy, And the
ceived next day, How could she treat me so? In-
felt quite sad To cause me such dis-tress; And

folks all stop and look a-round When-ev-er she goes by.
stead of be-ing mine for life She sim-ply an-swered "No."
when I said "Won't you be mine?" Of course she an-swered "Yes."

**Chorus**

Oh, I am as hap-py as a big sun-flower That

nods and bends in the breez - es, And my heart is as light as the

wind that blows The __ leaves from off the trees - es.

# The Gum-Tree Canoe

*Words by S. S. Steele • Music by A. F. Winnemore • 1847*

An old-time minstrel standby, this song is also called "Tombigbee River."
*When it was time for Laura to go to sleep in the covered wagon, the voice of the fiddle began
a long, swinging rhythm. As her eyelids closed she seemed to drift over endless seas of
prairie grasses to the sound of "Row away, row o'er the waters so blue." LHP, page 335*

1. On — Tom - big - bee Riv - er so bright I was
2. All the day in the field the soft cot - ton I

born, In a hut made of husks of the tall yel - low corn, And —
hoe, I — think of my Ju - lia and sing as I go, Oh, I

there I first met with my Ju - lia so true, And I
catch her a bird with a wing of true blue, And at

3. With my hands on the banjo and toe on the oar,
   I sing to the sound of the river's soft roar,
   While the stars they look down at my Julia so true
   And dance in her eye in our gum-tree canoe.

   (Chorus)

4. One night the stream bore us so far away
   That we couldn't come back so we thought we'd just stay,
   Oh, we spied a tall ship with a flag of true blue,
   And it took us in tow with our gum-tree canoe.

   (Chorus)

# A Railroad Man for Me

*Words and Music Traditional USA*

A "courting song," many examples of which are found in American folklore.
At Silver Lake, Laura and Lena met every morning and every evening to take
care of the cows. They led them to drink and moved the picket pins to fresh
grass; then they did the milking and sang. Sometimes they sang softly about
marrying a railroad man. *SSL, page* 48

**In jig tempo**

1. I would - n't mar - ry a farm - er, He's
2. I would - n't mar - ry a black - smith, He's

al - ways in the dirt,
al - ways in the black,

I'd rath - er mar - ry a
I'd rath - er mar - ry an

rail - road man Who wears a strip - ed shirt!
en - gi - neer That throws the throt - tle back.

**Chorus**

Oh, a rail - road man,___ a rail - road man, A

rail - road man for me! I'm going to mar - ry a

rail - road man, A rail-road-er's bride___ I'll be!_____

# My Heart Is Sair

# Barbary Allen

*Words and Music Traditional English*

This old ballad was brought to this country by the early colonists. There are many variants of the words and music, but the story remains essentially the same.

*Moonlight shone through the southern window and touched Pa's face and hands and the fiddle as the bow moved smoothly over the strings while he sang.*     SSL, *page 290*

**Simply, ballad style**

1. In Scar - let Town where I was born, There
2. All in the mer - ry month of May, When

was a fair maid dwell - in', ___ And ev - 'ry youth cried ___
green buds they were swell - in', ___ Young John - nie Grove on his

"Well - a - wa'" Her name was Bar - bary Al - len. ___
death - bed lay For love of Bar - bary Al - len. ___

3. He sent his man un - to her then, To the
4. (So) slow - ly, slow - ly, she came up, And

town where she did dwell in, — Say - ing "You must come to my
slow - ly she did came nigh him; — And all she said when

mas - ter If your name be Bar - bary Al - len." 4. So
there she came, "Young man, I think you're dy - ing."

5. He turned his face unto the wall,
And death was with him dealin',
"Adieu, adieu, to all my friends,
Adieu to Barbary Allen."

6. As she was walking o'er the fields,
She heard the bells aknellin',
And every stroke did seem to say
"Unworthy Barbary Allen."

7. When he was dead and laid in grave,
Her heart was struck with sorrow,
"O Mother, Mother, make my bed,
For I shall die tomorrow."

8. She on her deathbed as she lay
Begged to be buried by him,
And sore repented of the day
That she did e'er deny him.

9. "Farewell," she said, "ye virgins all,
And shun the fault I fell in,
Henceforth take warning by the fall
Of cruel Barbary Allen."

# Bonny Doon

*Words by Robert Burns • Traditional Scottish Tune • 1792*

In a letter written in 1794, Burns says this tune "was composed a good many years ago by an amateur playing on the black keys of the harpsichord."

*When everyone sang together in the surveyors' house at Silver Lake, Laura had never been so happy, and she was happiest of all when they were singing this plaintive air.*

SSL, *page 213*

1. Ye banks and braes of Bon - ny Doon, ___ How
2. Oft have I roved by Bon - ny Doon, ___ To

can ___ ye bloom ___ sae fresh ___ and fair? How ___ can ye chaunt, ye
see ___ the rose ___ and wood - bine twine, And ___ il - ka bird sang

lit - tle birds, ___ And I ___ sae wea - ry, full ___ of care?
of ___ its love, ___ And fond - ly sae ___ did I ___ o' mine.

Ye'll __ break my heart, __ ye lit - tle birds, __ That
Wi' __ light - some heart __ I pu'd a rose, __ Full

wan - ton through __ the flow - 'ring thorn, Ye __ mind me of __ de -
sweet __ up - on __ its thorn - y tree; But __ my false lov - er

part - ed joys, De - part - ed nev - er to __ re - turn.
stole __ the rose, And left __ the thorn __ be - hind __ wi' me.

# Highland Mary

*Words by Robert Burns • Traditional Scottish Tune • 1799*

Burns wrote to his friend George Thomson about the poem on which this song
is based: "It pleases myself; I think it is in my happiest manner." It appeared in
Thomson's *Scottish Airs*, set to the tune of "Katherine Ogle."
*This was Mary's favorite song. "It's sweet," she said. "It's sweet but it's sad," said Laura.*
SSL, *page* 154

1. Ye — banks and braes and streams a - round The — cas - tle o'— Mont - gom - er - y, Green — be your — woods and fair your flowers, Your — wa - ters — nev - er — drum - lie! There —
2. How — sweet - ly bloomed the gay green birk, How — rich the haw - thorn's blos - som, As — un - der - neath their fra - grant shade, I — clasped her — to — my — bos - om! The —

3. Wi' mony a vow and lock'd embrace,
   Our parting was fu' tender,
   And, pledging aft to meet again,
   We tore oursels asunder;
   But, oh, fell death's untimely frost,
   That nipped my flower sae early!
   Now green's the sod and cauld's the clay
   That wraps my Highland Mary!

4. Oh, pale, pale now those rosy lips
   I oft ha'e kiss'd sae fondly!
   And closed for aye the sparkling glance,
   That dwelt on me sae kindly!
   And mouldering now in silent dust,
   That heart that lo'ed me dearly;
   But still within my bosom's core
   Shall live my Highland Mary.

# Lily Dale

*Words and Music by H. S. Thompson • 1852*

This song is a favorite lament for a departed maiden. The melody became the theme for a schottische with variations, as well as for an ornate piano version.

*It was Christmas Eve in the sod house beside Plum Creek. Pa tuned the fiddle, rosined the bow, and sang about sweet Lily Dale.*

BPC, *page* 336

Andante, slowly and simply

1. 'Twas a calm, still night, And the moon's pale light Shone soft o'er hill and vale, When friends mute with grief Stood around the death-bed Of my poor lost Lily Dale.

2. "I go," she said, "To the land of rest, And ere my strength shall fail, I must tell you where Near my own loved home, You must lay poor Lily Dale."

**Chorus**

Oh! Lil - y, sweet Lil - y, dear Lil - y Dale, Now the wild rose blos - soms O'er her lit-tle green grave, 'Neath the trees in the flow - 'ry vale.

3. "'Neath the chestnut tree,
   Where the wild flowers grow,
   And the stream ripples forth through the vale,
   Where the birds shall warble
   Their songs in the spring
   There lay poor Lily Dale."

   (Chorus)

# My Heart Is Sair for Somebody

*Words by Robert Burns • Traditional Scottish Tune • 1796*

There may be echoes of Jacobite sentiment in this song, for James Stuart, the Old Pretender, was spoken of as "Somebody."

*The house on the prairie was full of Christmas plans and secrets; there were popcorn balls and little bags of candy in pink mosquito netting. Then Pa said, "Let's have a little music before we begin on these good things."*
HGY, page 226

Slowly, with expression

1. My heart is sair, I dare - na tell, My heart is sair for some - bod - y. O, I could wake a
2. Ye pow'rs that smile on vir - tuous love, O, sweet - ly smile on some - bod - y. Frae il - ka dan - ger

winter night,	A' for	the sake	o' some	-	bod - y!
keep	him free,	And send	me safe	my some	-	bod - y.

**Chorus**

O	-	hone!	for some	-	bod - y!

O	-	hey!	for some - bod - y!	I	could range	the
				I	would do,	what

world	a - round	For	the sake	o' some	-	bod - y.
would	I not,	For	the sake	o' some	-	bod - y?

# Kitty Wells

*Words by Thomas Sloan, Jr. • Music by Charles E. Atherton • Circa 1850*

Often called "Katy Wells," this song was handed down from memory in numerous versions. It was widely sung in rural areas of the United States.

*Laura and Mary were tucked in the trundle bed. Ma's hands were busy sewing by the lamplight. Pa was greasing his boots. He whistled cheerfully as he worked, and then he sang this ballad.*

LHBW, *page* 116

Moderately slow, with sentiment

1. You ask what caus-es me to weep, Why
2. I nev-er shall for-get the day That

he like oth-ers is not gay,  What makes the tear flow
we to-geth-er roamed the dells;  I kissed her cheek and

3. I often wish that I was dead
   And laid beside her in the tomb;
   The sorrow that bows down my head
   Is silent in the midnight gloom.
   The springtime has no charms for me
   Though flowers are blooming in the dells,
   For that bright form I do not see,
   'Tis the form of my sweet Kitty Wells.

   (Chorus)

# HYMNS AND SACRED SONGS

# We're All Here: The Song of
# the Freed Men

*Words and Music Traditional USA • 1880*

*Pa's fingers were too stiff from being out in the cold for him to play the fiddle. In hard times before, he had made music for them; now there was none for him. Suddenly Laura remembered the chorus of "The Song of the Freed Men." "We're all here!" she exclaimed. "We can sing!" And she began to hum the tune.* LW, *page 289*

Chorus

We're all here, we're all here, Do thy-self-a no harm; We're all here, we're all here, Do thy-self-a no harm.

3. As I go down the steps of time,
   Do thyselfa no harm,
   I leave this sinful world behind,
   Do thyselfa no harm.

   (Chorus)

4. If you get there before I do,
   Do thyselfa no harm,
   Tell them I am acoming too,
   Do thyselfa no harm.

   (Chorus)

# Am I a Soldier of the Cross?

*Words by Isaac Watts • Music by Reverend John Chetham • 1724*

Isaac Watts, an English Congregationalist pastor, wrote more than six hundred hymns. Many are still used today.

*On Sundays Laura and Mary could not run or shout or be noisy in their play. They had to sit quietly and hold their dolls or look at pictures. At bedtime Pa would play and sing "Shall I be carried to the skies. . . ."*

LHBW, *page 96*

1. Am I a sol - dier of the Cross, A fol - low'r of the Lamb? And shall I fear to own His cause Or blush to speak His name?

2. Shall I be car - ried to the skies On flow - 'ry beds of ease While oth - ers fought to win the prize And sailed through blood - y seas?

# When I Can Read My Title Clear

*Words by Isaac Watts • Music by J. P. Holbrook • 1799*

In addition to hymns and sermons, Isaac Watts was also the author of *Divine and Moral Songs for Children*, a celebrated book of juvenile verse.

*On the first night of the four-day blizzard on the prairie, the storm raged outside, hammering at the walls and windows. But the family, safely sheltered and huddled in the warmth of a hay fire, went on singing.*

LW, *page 290*

1. When I can read my ti - tle clear
2. Should earth a - gainst my soul en - gage,

To man - sions in the skies, I'll bid fare-
And hell - ish darts be hurled, Then I can

well to ev - 'ry fear And wipe my weep - ing eyes.
smile at Sa - tan's rage And face a frown - ing world.

3. Let cares like a wild deluge come,
   And storms of sorrow fall;
   May I but safely reach my home,
   My God, my heaven, my all.

4. There shall I bathe my weary soul
   In seas of heavenly rest,
   And not a wave of trouble roll
   Across my peaceful breast.

# The Home of the Soul

*Words by Mrs. E. H. Gates • Music by Philip Phillips • 1866*

At the composer's request, the words to this song were written in the spirit of *The Pilgrim's Progress*, the famous allegory by John Bunyan.

*The hymn blended with the wailing of the winds outside as Ma sat in her rocking chair and softly sang about the beautiful land "where no storms ever beat."*     LW, *page 241*

1. I will sing you a song of that beau-ti-ful land, The far-a-way home of the soul, Where no storms ev-er beat on the glit-ter-ing
2. Oh, the home of the soul! In my vi-sions and dreams, Its bright jas-per walls I can see; Till I fan-cy but dim-ly the veil in-ter-
3. Oh, how sweet it will be in that beau-ti-ful dream, So free from all sor-row and pain; With songs on our lips and with harps in our

strand While the years of e - ter - ni - ty roll.___
venes Be - tween the fair___ cit - y and me.___
hands, To meet one an - oth - er a - gain.___

**Chorus**

While___ the years of e - ter - ni - ty roll, Where no
Be ___ - tween the fair cit - y and me, Till I
To ___ meet one an - oth - er a - gain, With

storms ev - er beat on the glit - ter - ing
fan - cy but dim - ly the veil in - ter -
songs on our lips and with harps in our

strand While the years of e - ter - ni - ty roll.
venes Be - tween the fair___ cit - y and me.
hands To meet one an - oth - er a - gain.

# Merry, Merry Christmas!
## (*A Christmas Carol*)

*Words and Music by Mrs. T. J. Cook • 1871*

This carol has a hymnlike quality that makes it suitable for a church Christmas celebration like the wonderful one in Minnesota, where Laura saw her first Christmas tree and realized that everything on the tree was a present for someone!

SSL, *page* 187

ev - 'ry - where! Cheer - i - ly it ring - eth through the air.

**Verse**

1. Why should we so joy - ful - ly Sing with grate - ful mirth?
2. Light for wea - ry wan - der-ers, Com - fort for th' op-pressed!
3. Deeds of Faith and Char - i - ty, These our off -'rings be,

See, the Sun of Right - eous-ness Beams up - on the earth!
He will guide His trust - ing ones In - to per - fect rest.
Lead - ing ev - 'ry soul to sing Christ was born for me!

# My Sabbath Home

*Words by Dr. Christopher Ruby Blackall • Music by W. H. Doane • 1871*

The author, an army surgeon during the Civil War, wrote several Sunday-school songs in collaboration with W. H. Doane, who composed many hymns of the gospel type.

*Laura sang this at home when she was a little girl and later in a real Sunday-school class.*                                    BPC, *page* 298; HGY, *page* 41

Slowly, with sentiment

1. Sweet Sab - bath school more dear to me Than fair - est pal - ace dome, My heart e'er turns with joy to thee, My own dear Sab - bath Home.

2. Here first my will - ful, wan - d'ring heart The way of life was shown; Here first I sought the bet - ter part And gained a Sab - bath Home.

**Chorus**

Sab - bath Home! (Sweet Home!) Bless - ed Home! (Sweet Home!) Sab - bath

Home! (Sweet Home!) Bless-ed Home! (Sweet Home!) My heart e'er turns with

joy __ to __ thee, My own dear Sab - bath Home.

3. Here Jesus stands with loving voice,
Entreating me to come
And make of Him my earnest choice,
In this dear Sabbath Home.

(Chorus)

# The Ninety and Nine

*Words by Elizabeth D. Clephane • Music by Ira D. Sankey • 1876*

First published in an English magazine, this poem was little known until Ira D. Sankey came upon it and set it to music. It became the most famous of his gospel songs.

*In town everyone went to the revival meetings. There were hymns and prayers and preaching. Laura loved this hymn, but Reverend Brown's thunderous calls for repentance sent chills up her spine.*

LTP, *page 276*

1. There were nine-ty and nine that safe-ly lay, In the shel-ter of the fold, But one was out on the hills a-way, Far off from the gates of gold. A-

2. "Lord, Thou hast here Thy nine-ty and nine, Are they not e-nough for Thee?" But the Shep-herd made an-swer: "This of Mine Has wan-dered a-way from Me, And

way on the moun - tains wild and bare, A - way from the ten - der
al - though the road be rough and steep, I go to the des - ert to

Shep - herd's care, A - way from the ten - der Shep - herd's care.
find __ My sheep, I go to the des - ert to find __ My sheep."

3. But none of the ransomed ever knew
How deep were the waters crossed,
Nor how dark was the night that the Lord passed through
Ere He found His sheep that was lost.
Out in the desert He heard its cry,
Sick and helpless and ready to die,
Sick and helpless and ready to die.

4. "Lord, whence are those blood drops all the way
That mark out the mountain's track?"
"They were shed for one who had gone astray
Ere the Shepherd could bring him back."
"Lord, whence are Thy hands so rent and torn?"
"They are pierced tonight by many a thorn,
They are pierced tonight by many a thorn."

5. And all through the mountains, thunder-riven,
And up from the rocky steep
There rose a cry to the gate of Heaven,
"Rejoice! I have found My sheep!"
And the angels echoed around the throne,
"Rejoice, for the Lord brings back His own!
Rejoice, for the Lord brings back His own!"

# The Old Chariot

*Words and Music Traditional USA*

A Salvation Army favorite of long ago, this song was based on an African-American spiritual.

*During the long winter, Pa and some of the men in town set out in a railroad handcar to clear the tracks for the snowbound train. Everyone joined in singing this as they pushed the handlebars up and down.*

LW, *page* 107

**With movement and a strong beat**

**Chorus**

We'll roll the old char-iot a-long, We'll roll the old char-iot a-long, We'll roll the old char-iot a-long, And we won't drag on be-hind!

1. If the sin-ner's in the way, we will
2. If the Dev-il's in the way, we will

stop and take him in, ___ If the sin - ner's in the way, we will
roll it o - ver him, ___ If the Dev - il's in the way, we will

stop and take him in, ___ If the sin - ner's in the way, we will
roll it o - ver him, ___ If the Dev - il's in the way, we will

*D. C. al Fine*

stop and take him in, ___ And we won't drag on be - hind!
roll it o - ver him, ___ And we won't drag on be - hind!

# Sweet By and By

*Words by S. Fillmore Bennett • Music by J. P. Webster • 1867*

This "Christian ballad," written for a collection of Sunday-school hymns, was adopted by Ira D. Sankey for use as a revival number.

*After Sunday dinner, Pa played hymn tunes on his fiddle. They sang all afternoon while icy snow beat down upon the house.*

LW, *page* 130

1. There's a land that is fair - er than day, And by faith we can see it a - far, For the Fa - ther waits o - ver the way To pre - pare us a dwell - ing place there.

2. We shall sing on that beau - ti - ful shore The me - lo - di - ous songs of the blest, And our spir - its shall sor - row no more, Not a sigh for the bless - ing of rest.

3. To our bountiful Father above,
   We will offer the tribute of praise
   For the glorious gift of His love
   And the blessings that hallow our days.

   (Chorus)

# Pull for the Shore

*Words and Music by Philip Paul Bliss • Circa 1873*

The first words of this famous gospel song always made Laura want to laugh. She remembered how solemnly it had been sung by the tall thin man and the pudgy little one as they made their inebriated way from one to the other of De Smet's two saloons.

*LTP, pages 52, 278*

**Moderately**

1. Light in the dark-ness, sail-or, day is at hand!
2. Trust in the life-boat, sail-or, all else will fail;

See o'er the foam-ing bil-lows fair heav-en's land.
Strong-er the sur-ges dash, and fier-cer the gale;

Drear was the voy - age, sail - or, now al - most o'er;
Heed not the storm - y winds, though loud - ly they roar;

Safe with - in the life - boat, sail - or, pull for the shore.
Watch the bright and morn - ing star, and pull for the shore.

**Chorus**

Pull for the shore, sail - or, pull for the shore!

Heed not the roll - ing waves, but bend to the oar;

Safe in the life-boat, sail-or, cling to self no more;

Leave the poor old strand-ed wreck, and pull for the shore.

3. Bright gleams the morning, sailor; uplift the eye!
Clouds and darkness disappearing; glory is nigh!
Safe in the lifeboat, sailor, sing evermore,
Glory, glory, hallelujah! Pull for the shore!

(Chorus)

# There Is a Happy Land

*Words and Music by Reverend Andrew Young • 1838*

Andrew Young, a Scottish schoolmaster, wrote this beloved hymn for children.
*When Ma sang it, Laura didn't know she had fallen asleep. She thought shining angels had
begun to sing with Ma and that she was listening to their heavenly singing.*

LHP, *page* 220

1. There is a hap - py land, Far, far a - way, Where saints in glo - ry stand, Bright, bright as day. Oh, to hear the an - gels sing Glo - ry to the Lord, our King.

Loud    let    His    prais - es    ring,    Praise,    praise    for    aye.

2. Come to that happy land,
   Come, come away;
   Why will ye doubting stand,
   Why still delay?
   Oh, we shall happy be
   When from sin and sorrow free,
   Lord, we shall live with Thee,
   Blest, blest for aye.

3. Bright, in that happy land,
   Beams every eye;
   Kept by a Father's hand,
   Love cannot die.
   Oh, then to glory run;
   Be a crown and kingdom won,
   And bright above the sun,
   We reign for aye.

# INDEX

Song titles are listed in capital letters, first lines of songs in upper-and-lowercase roman.
First lines as they appear in the Little House books are in upper-and-lowercase italic.